The Wedding Tradition

" I take thee to my wedded husband (wife)
to have and to hold from this day forward
for better or worse
for richer or poorer
in sickness and in health
to love and to cherish till death do us part
according to Gods' holy ordinance
and thereto I give thee my troth."

Marriage is the intimate sharing of two lives. A good and balanced relationship is one in which neither person is overpowered or absorbed by the other. Marriage requires periods of aloneness so the individuality of each partner can continue to be distinctive and deepen. Each is the guardian of the others' solitude. To affirm the distance between each other is to affirm the dignity and friendship which helps the other grow.

The wedding ceremony does not join two people; they do that through their awareness of the bond already in existence. The ceremony proclaims the fact. Invited relatives and friends have the opportunity to emotionally support the couple in the vows they choose or the ones they choose to create.

MARRIAGE

Love is a power that liberates the potential for morality. It has nothing to do with finding the right person and everything to do with generating the conditions under which one expresses his or her real self. Marriage requires this kind of environment: where two people make a passionate effort to become the embodiment of truth.

A FEW IDEAS

- I pledge to share my life openly with you.

- I promise to encourage your fulfillment as an individual through the changes of our lives.

- I vow to fulfill my human potential and support you in fulfilling yours.

- I want to live with you just as you are.

- I promise to give you the space to be and grow.

- I promise to be honest with myself and therefore you.

- I promise to be faithful to our commitment to share our lives.

- I promise to invest in our friendship and communicate my feelings.

- I vow to live within our means and seek elegance instead of luxury, refinement rather than fashion and wealth instead of riches.

- I vow to never take you for granted and to be grateful for the chance to share my life with you.

- I promise to fall in love with you many times.

- I promise to be kind, and when I am wrong admit it.

- I promise to be affectionate, and when I am right be kind.

- My commitment to you is for all of my life.

PHOTO: COMPLIMENTS OF CINDY AND MARK RUFFNER

Ribbons and Bows

Loopy Bow

You can vary the basic loopy bow by adding extra loops and tails before you wire the center together; staggering the length of the tails, or exaggerating the width of the bow. Add some decorative detail to the center with a glue gun or wire.

1 Cross ribbon ends making the tails as long and the bow as wide as you want. Where the ribbon crosses is the center of the bow.

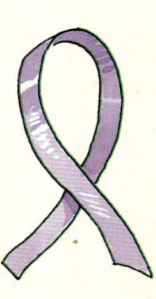

2 Bring the center to the crossed tails and pinch the bow together. Secure the center with a small piece of floral wire.

3 Cut the tails at an angle or in points to finish off the look of the bow.

Wiring Stems

By wiring the stems together the flowers and ferns are held securely in place. It also adds flexibility to the "handle" of the project allowing it to bend.

1 Loosely wrap the wire around the full length of the stems in a spiral.

2 Cut stems even across the bottom before taping.

Taping Wired Stems

1 Wrap a piece of floral tape around the top of the wire and press in place.

2 Turn the stems while stretching and pulling the tape in a downward angle. The tape should be tightly wrapped around the wired stems without buckles or gaps.

COVER WIRED STEMS WITH FLORAL TAPE

Wrapping Stems with Ribbon

1 Hot glue the end of the ribbon 1" from the bottom of the stems.

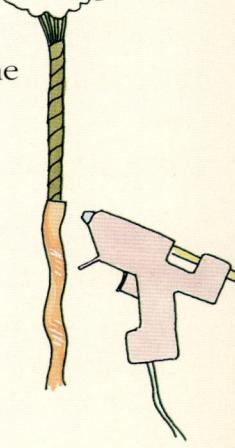

2 Pull the ribbon around the bottom of the stems and wrap carefully up the length of the stems. Hot glue at the top to secure and trim off any extra ribbon.

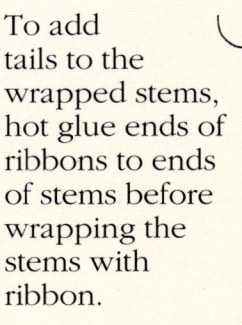

To add tails to the wrapped stems, hot glue ends of ribbons to ends of stems before wrapping the stems with ribbon.

FLORIST BOW

1 Measure the length of one of the ribbon tails, and with the right side of the ribbon on the outside, make a loop and squeeze the ribbon together. Hold it with your thumb and forefinger.

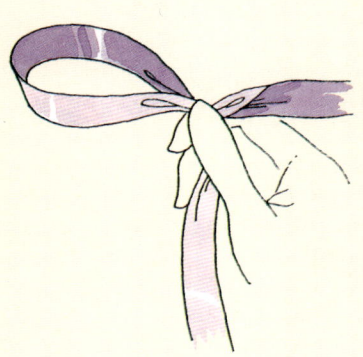

2 Make a full twist of the ribbon so the right side is facing out.

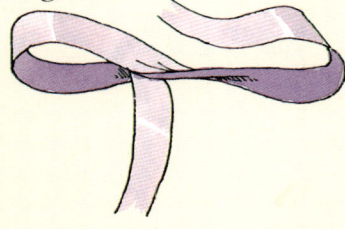

3 Make another loop toward the other side.

4 Make a slightly smaller set of loops on top of the first set of loops. Continue to alternate the loops, right and left, until you have made as many as you like.

5 To complete the bow, twist the remaining ribbon around your thumb to make the center loop. The remaining ribbon is the second tail. Adjust both tails so the ribbon is on the right side. Put a small piece of wire through the center of the top loop, and twist it tightly at the back of the bow to hold all the loops together. The wire should be tight enough to hold the loops, but loose enough so you can move the loops to create a full, fluffy bow.

6 Spread out the bow loops and trim the ends of the tails.

THE RECEPTION ARRANGEMENT

Materials

- 1-12" Vase
- 1 Floral foam
- 3 Stems (peach) delphiniums
- 4 Stems (peach) blossom branches
- 2 Stems (purple) blossom branches
- 7 Stems (peach) open roses
- 3 Stems (white) open roses
- 5 Stems (purple) hydrangeas
- 3 Stems (white) snowballs X2
- 2 Stems (white) wild rose
- 3 Stems (purple) fat lilacs
- 2 Stems (pink) fat lilacs
- 4 Stems (pink) thin lilacs
- 6 Stems tree fern (preserved)
- 6 Stems plumosa fern (preserved)
- 2 Yds. (peach) 2" wired ribbon
- 1 Floral pick

Tools

- Wire cutters
- Serrated knife
- Scissors

Instructions

1 Cut foam to fit inside vase snugly.

2 Insert the tallest stems first to determine the shape of arrangement.

3 Taper the flowers down and fill out the arrangement with roses and lilacs.

4 Fill in the empty spaces with the preserved fern.

5 Make a ten inch wide, 4 loop (loopy) bow with 11" tails and wire to floral pick. *(See page 4)* Insert in front of arrangement.

BRIDES' HAT

Materials

- 1-17" (Ivory) hat
- 1 Stem (white) open rose with bud
- 1 Stem (white) open rose with leaves
- 1 Stem (white) snowball
- 1 Yd. (white) netting
- 1/3 Yd (white) dotted netting
- 1-2/3 Yds. 2" wide (white) sheer ribbon with gold edge
- 24" String of large pearls

Tools

- Wire cutter
- Hot glue gun/glue sticks
- Scissors

Instructions

1 Glue rim of hat half way to bottom of crown.

2 Hot glue pearls around bottom of crown.

3 Cut the large open rose with bud stem to 2" and hot glue over glued spot where rim is turned and glued.

4 Hot glue the second open rose with leaves below it facing the back of the hat.

5 Cut snowball in half and glue one piece below the second rose

6 Cut an 8 X 36" strip of dotted netting and make a twelve inch wide, 2 loop (loopy) bow with 10" tails. *(See page 4.)* Hot glue under snowball flowers with loops at an angle facing the crown.

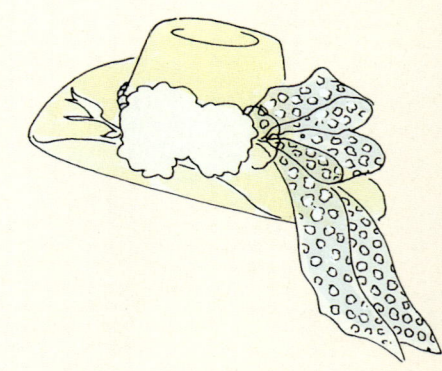

7 Cut four 36 X 8" wide strips of plain netting. Wire the tops of the strips together and hot glue to hat (going towards the back) next to dotted bow

8 Make the sheer ribbon into an eight inch wide, 2 loop (loopy) bow with 19" tails and glue on top of plain netting streamers.

LACE GARTER

Materials

- 1- Lace fringed garter
- 1 (Pink) rose bud
- 1 Small piece of snowball
- 1 small piece of plumosa fern
- 24" (white) 2" sheer ribbon with gold edge
- Floral wire

Tools

- Glue gun/glue sticks
- Wire cutters

Instructions

1 Make a five inch wide, 2 loop (loopy) bow with long tails out of the sheer ribbon. *(See page 4.)*

2 Glue rose bud to center of bow.

3 Add small piece of snowball and plumosa fern around the rose bud.

4 Glue the ribbon with the florals onto the garter.

Materials

- 3 Stems plumosa fern (preserved)
- 2 Stems (pink) tight rose buds
- 2 Stems maidenhair fern (silk)
- 2 Stems (white) paper roses with buds
- 2 Stems (white) large open roses
- 3 Stems (white) medium roses
- 2 Stems (white) snowballs
- 1/3 Yd. (or 5 X 8") (white) dotted netting
- 2 Yds. (white) 2" sheer ribbon with gold edges
- 1 Yd. (green) 2" sheer ribbon
- 1/2 Yd. (tapestry) 2" ribbon
- 1 Yd. (gold) 1/4" ribbon
- Floral wire
- Floral tape

Tools

- Wire cutters
- Scissors
- Glue gun/glue sticks

Instructions

1 Place the bear grass, maidenhair, and plumosa fern in your hand.

2 Arrange the roses, rosebuds and paper roses on top of the greenery. Cut the snowball in half and add to the arrangement. Keep the flowers very close together.

3 Wire the stems together to form a handle. Cut the stems, even at the bottom, to 6-1/2" and cover the stems with floral tape. *(See page 4.)*

4 Cut a 5 X 8" strip of dotted netting. Set aside.

5 Using the white and gold edged ribbon, make a ten inch wide, 4 loop florist bow with 17" tails. *(See page 5.)*

6 Wire the white bow to the middle of the sheer green ribbon. Wire the white bow with the green streamers to the middle of the piece of dotted netting. Set aside.

7 Wrap the handle with tapestry ribbon. *(See page 4.)*

8 Wire the layered ribbons to the top of the stems under the lowest leaves. Tie the thin gold ribbon in a knot around the top of the stems.

The Bridal Bouquet
(To Throw)

Materials

- 2 Stems plumosa fern
- 3 Stems bear grass (preserved)
- 2 Stems (white) paper roses
- 2 Stems (white) open silk roses
- 2 Stems (white/green) snowballs
- 1 Stem (white/green) lilac
- 1-1/3 Yds. (white/gold edged) 2" sheer ribbon
- 1 Small piece (5 X 6") (white) dotted netting
- 1-1/3 Yds. (white) 2" sheer ribbon
- 1 Yd. (green) 2" sheer ribbon
- Floral tape
- Floral wire

Tools

- Wire cutters
- Glue gun/glue sticks

Instructions

1 Cut the leaves in 3 leaf sections from all the flowers, and cut the flower and fern stems to 7".

2 Wire or tape a 3 leaf stem below each of the flower heads.

3 Hold the two silk roses in your hand and surround them with some of the plumosa and all of the bear grass.

4 Add the remaining flowers around the center roses and add the rest of the plumosa fern in-between the flowers.

5 Add any remaining leaves around the outside of the arrangement. Cut all stems even with the first cut stems. Wire the stems together and wrap with floral tape. *(See page 4.)*

6 Cut a 7" piece of green ribbon and hot glue it to the end of the stems. Wrap the stems with the green ribbon leaving a six inch tail. *(See page 4.)*

7 Make two eight inch wide, 2 loop (loopy) bows with 16" tails using the white sheer ribbon and the gold edged ribbon. *(See page 4.)*

8 Layer the two bows on top of the dotted netting and wire all three together. Wire bows and netting to the top of the stems under the lowest leaves.

Boutonnieres' for Groom & Best Man

Materials

- 1 Stem (white) partly open rose bud
- 1 Stem plumosa fern
- Floral tape
- Floral wire

Tools

- Wire cutters

Instructions:

1 Cut rose bud stem to 1-1/2".

2 Cut top piece of fern to 5" long.

3 Lay rose bud on top of fern and wire the two stems together. Cover the wire with floral tape. *(See page 4.)*

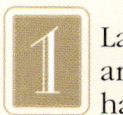

MAID OF HONOR BOUQUET

Materials

- 4 Stems bear grass (preserved)
- 2 Stems tree fern (preserved)
- 2 Stems plumosa fern (preserved)
- 1 Stem (purple) blossoms
- 1 Stem (peach) blossoms
- 1 Stem (purple) lilac
- 1 Stem (white) snowball
- 3 Stems (pink) open roses
- 3 Yds. (peach) 2" wired ribbon
- 1 Yd (pink) 2" sheer ribbon
- 1/3 Yd. (pink) dotted netting
- Floral wire
- Floral tape

Tools

- Wire cutters
- Scissors
- Hot glue gun/glue sticks

Instructions

1 Lay bear grass, tree fern and plumosa in your hand.

2 Arrange the blossom branches, lilacs, snow balls and roses on top of the greenery. Place them very close together.

3 Cut the stems to 9" long and wire them together. Cover the wire with floral tape. *(See page 4.)*

4 Cut a 36 X 5" strip of dotted netting and make a 12" wide, 2 loop (loopy) bow with 8" tails. *(See page 4.)* Set aside.

5 Using the peach ribbon, make an eight inch wide, 2 loop (loopy) bow with 8" tails. Set aside.

6 Cut the sheer ribbon in half and hot glue the ends of the ribbons to the end of the stems. Cut two 24" pieces of the peach ribbon and hot glue the ends to the end of the stems. *(See page 5.)*

7 Wrap the wired stems with the remaining peach ribbon.

8 Wire the peach bow to the dotted bow, and wire the dotted bow to the top of the stems close to the bottom flowers.

Materials

- 2 Stems (purple) delphiniums
- 1 Stem (white) snowball
- 8 Stems (pink) open roses
- 1 Stem (white) large open rose
- 6 Stems (purple) hydrangeas
- 2 Stems (peach) blossoms
- 2 Stems (purple) blossoms
- 4 Stems (purple) lilacs
- 4 Stems (pink) wild roses
- 8 Stems plumosa fern (preserved)
- 8 Stems bear grass (preserved)
- 6 Stems tree fern (preserved)
- 2 Yds. 1/8" (pink) ribbon
- 1 Yd. (pink) dotted netting
- 12 Yds. (white) 3" ribbon
- 3 Yds. (green) 2" sheer ribbon
- 2 Yds. (pink) 2" sheer ribbon
- 1-2/3 Yds. iridescent netting
- Floral wire
- Floral tape

Tools:

- Wire cutters
- Scissors

Note: Make two bouquets and wire them together. Wire them to the middle of the arch. Cover the center with extra flowers.

Instructions

FOR ONE BOUQUET

1 Hold four stems of bear grass, three stems of tree fern and 4 stems of plumosa fern in your hand.

2 Arrange 1/2 of the materials over the greenery. (Set aside the snowball and large open rose.) Layer the flowers to extend the bouquet to two feet. Use floral wire to bind the stems together.

3 Wire the stems at the bottom of the bouquet and cover them with floral tape. *(See page 4.)*

4 Cut the 1/8" ribbon in half and tie one piece around the top of the stems close to the bottom flowers.

5 Cut the sheer pink and green ribbons in half and tie one piece of each around the top of the stems, on top of the 1/8" ribbon.

6 Cut a 36 X 8" strip of dotted netting and make a twelve inch wide, 2 loop (loopy) bow with 6" tails. *(See page 4.)* Set aside.

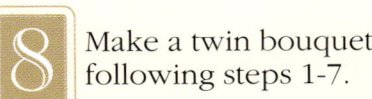

7 Cut a 52 X 6" wide strip of iridescent netting and make a twelve inch wide, 2 loop (loopy) bow with one 12" tail and one 16" tail. *(See page 4.)* Wire the dotted bow to the net bow and the net bow (with the dotted bow) to the top of the stems over the other ribbons.

8 Make a twin bouquet following steps 1-7.

9 Wire the ends of each of the garlands, with the stems facing each other and overlapping about 6-8".

10 Wire the combined "bouquets" to the top front of the arch. Add the remaining snowball and rose to the center of the arrangement to cover the stems.

11 Wire the middle of the wide, white ribbon to the top of the arch in back of the flowers, and weave through the lattice arch in graceful loops down to each pedestal.

PEDESTAL DECORATION

Materials

- 2 Stems (purple) delphinium
- 2 Stems (pink) delphinium
- 12 Stems (purple) hydrangeas
- 6 Stems (white) snowballs
- 6 Stems (white) lilacs
- 2 Stems (white) large open roses
- 4 Stems (pink) medium open roses
- 6 Stems plumosa fern (preserved)
- 6 Stems tree fern (preserved)
- Floral tape
- Floral wire

Tools

- Wire cutters
- Scissors

Instructions

1 Divide the materials in half. Arrange a bouquet of flowers in your hand starting with the roses in the center and some of the plumosa and tree fern around the roses.

2 Add the remaining flowers to the bouquet. Place the remaining portions of the ferns on the outside of the arrangement.

3 Wire the stems and cover the wire with floral tape. *(See page 4.)*

4 Make a twin bouquet with the remaining materials for the second pedestal.

5 Insert the stems of each bouquet through the top of the open pedestals and spread the flowers apart so they fill in the empty space between the pedestals and the lattice arch.

6 Thread the tail of the white, wide ribbon from the center arch through each side of the pedestal flowers.

Bridesmaids' Hat

Materials

- 1-15" (Pink) hat
- 1 Stem (peach) open rose
- 1 Stem (purple) lilac
- 1 Stem (pink) small rose X2
- 1 Yd. (pink) dotted netting
- 2 Yds. (or 22 X 72") (pink) netting
- 1-1/2 Yds. (pink) sheer 2" ribbon
- 1 Stem (purple) hydrangea
- 5 Stems (pink) small rosebuds
- Floral Wire

Tools

- Glue gun/glue sticks
- Wire cutters
- Scissors

Instructions

1 Cut a 22 X 72" strip of plain netting. Wire six, equal gathered sections and glue to hat at even intervals.

2 Cut 5 hydrangea florettes and glue one over each of the glued down, wired puffs. Add one rosebud under each of the hydrangea florettes.

3 Cut a 5 X 36" strip of dotted netting and make a nine inch wide, 2 loop (loopy) bow with 9" tails. *(See page 4.)* Set aside.

4 Make a seven inch wide, 2 loop (loopy) bow with 10" tails from the sheer ribbon.

5 Wire the sheer bow to the center of the dotted bow and hot glue the dotted bow to the center back of the hat.

6 Cut the open rose stem to 1" and glue to top of ribbon. Cut the lilac and remaining rose stems to 1" and glue around open rose under the ribbon.

Bridesmaids' Bouquet

Materials

- 4 Stems bear grass (preserved)
- 2 Stems tree fern (preserved)
- 1 Stem plumosa fern
- 1 Stem (purple) lilac
- 1 Stem (pink) open rose
- 1 Stem (white) snowball
- 3 Yd. (peach) 2" wired ribbon
- 1 Yd. (pink) sheer 2" ribbon
- 1 Yd. (or 36 X 5") (pink) dotted netting
- Floral wire
- Floral tape

Tools

- Wire cutters
- Scissors
- Hot glue gun/glue sticks

Instructions

1 Remove leaves from flowers.

2 Layer the bear grass, tree fern and plumosa fern in your hand. Arrange the open rose, lilac and snowball on top of the greenery.

3 Wire the stems together and cut stems even on the bottom to 9" long. Cover with floral tape *(See page 4.)*

4 Cut a 5 X 36" strip of dotted netting and make a twelve inch wide, 2 loop (loopy) bow with 7" tails. *(See page 4.)* Set aside.

5 Using the peach ribbon, make an eight inch wide, 2 loop (loopy) bow with 8" tails. Set aside.

6 Cut the sheer ribbon in half and hot glue the ends of the two pieces to the end of the stems. Cut two 20" pieces from the peach ribbon and hot glue the ends to the end of the stems. *(See page 4).*

7 Wrap the stems with the remaining peach wired ribbon.

8 Wire the peach bow to the dotted bow and wire the dotted bow to the top of the stems close to the bottom flowers.

Materials

- 3 Stems (pink) blossoms
- 1 Stem (pink) open rose
- 1 Stem (purple) hydrangea
- 1 Stem (white) snowball
- 1-1/2 Yds. (green) 2" sheer ribbon
- 1-1/2 Yds. (white with gold edging) 2" sheer ribbon
- 1 Yd. (pink) 2" sheer ribbon
- Floral wire

Tools:

- Glue gun/glue sticks
- Wire cutters
- Scissors

Instructions

1 Cut blossom stems at bottom of last flower.

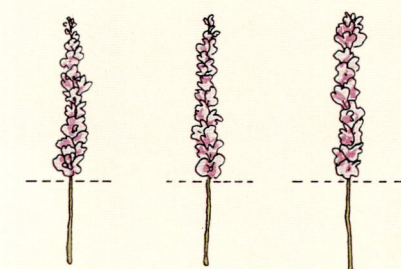

2 Wire the remaining flower stems together to form a 23" circle (or a circle to fit the size of the head).

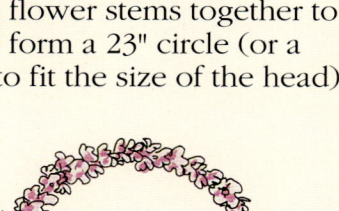

3 Hot glue the open rose over a place where the flower stems meet. Hot glue pieces of snowball and a few hydrangea flowers around the rose.

4 Randomly glue hydrangea florets onto blossom garland.

5 Make a seven inch wide, 2 loop (loopy) bow with one 24" tail and one 12" tail with the white ribbon and another one just like it with the green ribbon. (See page 4.) Set aside.

6 Make a four inch wide, 2 loop (loopy) bow with one 19" tail and one 9" tail with the sheer pink ribbon.

7 Wire the pink bow to the green bow; and the green bow to the white one. Wire the white one (and the layer of bows) to the garland very close to the open rose.

Flower Girl Basket

Materials

- 1-8 X 3" Oval basket
- 24" (Pink) heavy thread
- Needle
- 1-1/2 Yds. 1/8" (green) ribbon
- 1/3 Yd. (pink) dotted netting
- 1 Yd. (pink) 2" sheer ribbon
- 1 Stem (pink) rose
- 1 Stem (white) snowball
- 1 Stem (purple) lilac
- 1 Stem plumosa fern
- Florist wire

Tools

- Wire cutters
- Glue gun/glue sticks
- Scissors

Instructions

1 Cut a 36 X 6" strip of dotted netting. Run a gathering stitch down the middle.

2 Wire the ruffled netting to one end of the handle. Cover the top of the handle with the ruffles and wire to other end of handle. Adjust gathers.

3 Cut the thin ribbon in half and tie a shoelace bow with one of the ribbons around the netting and the handle 1/3 of the way up. Do the same on the other side.

4 Cut a 6 X 12" piece of netting. (Set aside.) Using the pink sheer ribbon, make a seven inch wide, 2 loop (loopy) bow with 8-10" tails. *(See page 4.)* Wire center of bow to center of netting. Wire both to bottom of handle.

5 Glue one rose; part of the lilac and 1/3 of the snowball and fern to basket on top of the center of the bow.

MOTHER'S CORSAGE

Materials

- *1 Stem (white) open rose with bud*
- *1 Stem (white) snowball*
- *1 Stem plumosa fern (preserved)*
- *3 Stems bear grass (preserved)*
- *4 X 5" piece of dotted netting*
- *1/2 Yd. (white) 2" sheer ribbon*
- *1/2 Yd (mossy green) 2" sheer ribbon*
- *Floral wire*
- *Floral tape*

Tools

- *Wire cutters*
- *Scissors*

Instructions

1 Hold the flower bud in your left hand. Place open rose below bud.

2 Add small pieces of snowball to the right and left of the open rose.

3 Add the top 8" of the plumosa stem and the top 10" of the bear grass to bottom of arrangement.

4 Wire the stems together close to the bottom of the big rose. Cut all the stems to 2" and cover the stems with floral tape. *(See page 4.)*

5 Make two, one loop bows with 8" tails out of the sheer ribbons.

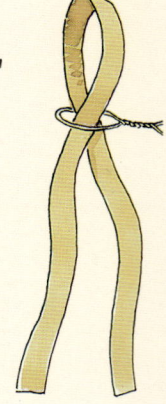

6 Lay the one loop bows on top of the dotted netting and wire the three together.

7 Wire the ribbon section to the stems beneath the open rose.

THE BRIDAL CENTERPIECE

Materials

- 1- 6" Decorative pot
- 1-5" Ivy topiary with 4 candle holders
- 4-6" (White) candles
- 3 Stems (white) wild roses
- 1 Yd. (peach) 2" wired ribbon
- 1/3 Yd. (pink) dotted netting
- 1/3 Yd. (white with gold edges) 2" sheer ribbon
- Floral wire
- Floral tape

Tools

- Wire cutters
- Scissors

Instructions

1 Cut a 6 X 36" strip of dotted netting and make a twelve inch wide 2 loop (loopy) bow with 6" tails. *(See page 4.)* Set aside.

2 Using the peach ribbon, make a six inch wide, 4 loop florist bow with 4" tails. *(See page 5.)* Set aside.

3 Cut the rose stems to 6" and wire them together. Cover the stems with floral tape. *(See page 4.)*

4 Wire the peach bow to the dotted net bow, and wire both of the bows to the middle of the sheer white ribbon with the gold edges. Wire the layered ribbons to the top of the stems underneath the roses.

5 Insert the covered stems into the potted ivy. Fluff up the bows.

THE WEDDING CAKE

Materials

- 1 Plastic cake top
- 1 Cherub (or bride and groom etc.)
- 1 Stem (white) large rose
- 1 Stem (pink) medium rose
- 1 Small piece (white) lilac
- 1 Small piece (purple) lilac
- 1 Stem plumosa fern
- 1/3 Yd. (pink) dotted netting
- 1 Yd. (pink) 2" sheer ribbon

Tools:

- Wire cutter
- Glue gun/glue sticks
- Scissors

Instructions

1 Hot glue cherub (or bride and groom) to middle front of cake top.

2 Cut flower stems to 3". Glue pink rose on left side of "cherub", lilac pieces to right of pink rose and large white rose in back of "cherub".

3 Hot glue leaves and plumosa around "cherub" and flowers.

4 Cut a 6 X 36" strip of dotted netting and make a twelve inch wide 2 loop (loopy) bow with 6" tails. *(See page 4.)* Hot glue to cake top in back of flowers.

5 Glue the middle of the sheer ribbon (streamers) to the cake top under the flowers in front.

Materials

- 3 Stems bear grass (preserved)
- 3 Stems tree fern (preserved)
- 2 Stems plumosa fern (preserved)
- 1 Stem (purple) blossoms
- 1 Stem (peach) blossoms
- 1 Stem ((white) large rose with bud
- 1 Stem (pink) medium open rose
- 2 Stems (purple) hydrangeas
- 1 Stem (purple) lilac
- 2-2/3 Yds. (iridescent) netting
- 2 Yds. (green) 2" sheer ribbon
- 1 Yd. (pink) 2" sheer ribbon
- 1 Yd. (pink) 1/8" ribbon
- 1/3 Yd. (pink) dotted netting
- Floral wire
- Floral tape

Tools

- Wire cutters
- Scissors

Instructions

1 Hold a layer of bear grass, tree fern and plumosa fern in your hand.

2 Arrange the blossoms, roses, hydrangeas and lilac on top of the greenery. Keep the flowers close together.

3 Cut the stems to 5" and wire them together. Cover them with floral tape. *(See page 4.)*

4 Cut a 6 X 36" strip of dotted netting. Make a twelve inch wide, 2 loop (loopy) bow with 6" tails. *(See page 4.)* Set aside.

5 Cut a 72 X 7" strip of the iridescent netting and make a twelve inch wide, 4 loop (loopy) bow with a 21" tail and a 27" tail. Set aside.

6 Tie the green sheer ribbon and the thin pink ribbon in a knot around the top of the stems.

7 Wire the dotted bow to the iridescent bow. Wire the iridescent bow on top of the knotted ribbons.

8 Bend the stems to form a hanging loop.

FLOWER GIRLS' SWAG

Materials

- 1-38" Plumosa garland
- 1 Stem (pink) open rose
- 2 Stems (purple) hydrangeas
- 3 Stems (white) hydrangeas
- 2 Stems (white) wild roses X2
- 2 Yds. (pink) 2" sheer ribbon
- 1/3 Yd. (pink) dotted netting
- 4 Yds. (peach) 2" wired ribbon
- 2 Yds. (green) 1/4" ribbon
- Floral wire

Tools:

- Glue gun/glue sticks
- Wire cutters
- Scissors

Note: If you can't find a ready made plumosa garland, buy several packages of plumosa stems and wire them together to form a 32" long garland.

Instructions

1 Cut pink rose stem to 2". Lay garland flat and hot glue to center of swag.

2 Cut flower heads of two white hydrangeas into groups of 3-4 flowers. Hot glue around the pink rose.

3 Cut wild roses into single stems (2" long) and hot glue two around the pink rose and two at either end in the back of the garland.

4 Cut remaining flower heads from the white and purple hydrangeas leaving 1/2" stems, and randomly glue all over garland, front and back.

5 Cut two 6 X 36" strips of dotted netting, and make two, twelve inch wide, 2 loop (loopy) bows with 6" tails. *(See page 4.)* Set aside.

6 Using the peach ribbon, make two twelve inch, 2 loop (loopy) bows with 6" tails.

7 Cut the sheer ribbon and the remaining peach ribbon in half and wire a piece of each ribbon to each bow for streamers.

8 Wire the ribbons with the streamers to the ends of the swag.

9 Cut the thin ribbon in half and tie to each end of the swag above the bows.